Bipolar Disorder

Perspectives on Mental Health

by Judith Peacock

Consultant:
Valerie J. Williams, LCSW
Wholistic Therapy Services
Geneva, Illinois

LifeMatters
an imprint of Capstone Press
Mankato, Minnesota

LifeMatters Books are published by Capstone Press
PO Box 669 • 151 Good Counsel Drive • Mankato, Minnesota 56002
http://www.capstone-press.com

Printed in the United States of America

Library of Congress Cataloging-in-Publication Data
Peacock, Judith, 1942-
　　　　Bipolar disorder / by Judith Peacock.
　　　　　　　　p.　　　cm. — (Perspectives on mental health)
　　　　Includes bibliographical references and index.
　　　　Summary: Explains bipolar disorder including its types, diagnosis, and treatment and offers strategies for dealing with this illness in oneself and others.
　　　　ISBN 0-7368-0434-X (book) — ISBN 0-7368-0440-4 (series)
　　　　1. Manic-depressive illness—Juvenile literature.　2. Depression, Mental—Juvenile literature. 3. Affective disorders—Juvenile literature. [1. Manic-depressive illness. 2. Depression, Mental. 3. Affective disorders.] I. Title. II. Series.
　　　　RC516 .P43 2000
　　　　616.89´5—dc21　　　　　　　　　　　　　　　　　　99-056078
　　　　　　　　　　　　　　　　　　　　　　　　　　　　　　CIP

Staff Credits
Marta Fahrenz, editor; Adam Lazar, designer; Jodi Theisen, photo researcher

Photo Credits
Cover: ©Capstone Press/Adam Lazar
FPG International/©Telegraph Colour Library, 10; ©Jeff Kaufman, 28; ©Eric O'Connell, 38; ©Jill Sabella, 41
Index Stock/27
International Stock/©Scott Barrow, 13; ©Tom Till, 20; ©Don Romero, 59
Photo Network/©D. L. Baldwin, 25; ©Esbin-Anderson, 42; ©Jeff Greenberg, 55
Photri Inc./17, 49
PNI/©StockByte, 8
Unicorn Stock/©Jay Foreman, 7; ©Jeff Greenberg, 19; ©Eric R. Berndt, 51
Visuals Unlimited/©Mark E. Gibson, 33

Table of Contents

1	What Is Bipolar Disorder?	4
2	Types of Bipolar Disorder	14
3	How Is Bipolar Disorder Diagnosed?	22
4	Bipolar Disorder in Children and Teens	34
5	How Is Bipolar Disorder Treated?	44
6	Staying Healthy	52
	Glossary	60
	For More Information	61
	Useful Addresses and Internet Sites	62
	Index	63

Chapter
Overview

People with bipolar disorder alternate between two opposite and extreme emotions. Their mood swings back and forth from excessively happy, or high, to sad and hopeless.

During episodes of mania, people with bipolar disorder are full of energy. They feel excited and restless. They also may be irritable.

During episodes of depression, people with bipolar disorder have constant feelings of sadness and hopelessness. They lack energy and may lose the ability to function in daily life.

Bipolar disorder is an illness that involves the brain. Most people who have this illness have a relative with a mood disorder.

If left untreated, bipolar disorder can upset a person's life. The disease can be hard on family members and friends as well.

Chapter 1

What Is Bipolar Disorder?

Everyone has highs and lows, ups and downs, good days and bad days. Mood changes are normal. However, the mood changes of the illness bipolar disorder are extreme. Doctors identify bipolar disorder as a mood disorder.

People who have bipolar disorder experience extreme changes in mood, energy, and behavior. They alternate, or switch, between two opposite emotions. *(Bi* means "two" and *polar* means "opposite.")* Their mood repeatedly alternates from extremely happy, or high, to sad and hopeless. In between the extremes, their mood might be calm. People with bipolar disorder cannot control their mood changes.

People with unipolar disorder experience one extreme emotion—sadness. *Uni* means "one." Unipolar disorder is another name for major depression.

Jamie is a smart and talented high school senior. He writes

JAMIE, AGE 17

music and has his own band. Jamie can be very friendly but also very moody. Sometimes, for no reason, he feels tired and sad. Then, just as unexpectedly, he feels full of life and energy. Sometimes he feels intensely angry.

These extreme mood changes upset Jamie. They make him feel out of control. He thinks about hurting himself or someone else. Jamie's thoughts frighten him even more.

Jamie has started drinking to calm his emotions. He also uses marijuana, which is often available when his band plays at parties.

Bipolar disorder has four categories, or types, that range from mild to serious. A general description of bipolar disorder follows. The categories are described in Chapter 2.

A Roller Coaster of Highs and Lows

People with bipolar disorder ride an emotional roller coaster. They soar high and then plunge low. These mood extremes are called episodes. The high times are called mania. The low times are called depression. Each episode can last from a few weeks to several months. Manic depression is another name for bipolar disorder.

The episodes of bipolar disorder vary in pattern, length, and frequency. These differences influence how a person is affected by bipolar disorder. They also influence treatment for the disease.

The highs and lows can be terrifying for people with bipolar disorder. Many people with undiagnosed, or unidentified, bipolar disorder don't understand why they feel the way they do. They often are unhappy, angry, and frustrated with feeling emotionally out of control.

Mania—The Highs

During a manic episode, people with bipolar disorder may feel excited and restless. They feel like they are on top of the world. Nothing, not even bad news, can change their happiness. They have intense energy and may go for days without sleep. They have countless ideas for things they want to achieve. Thoughts race through their mind, and they talk rapidly. They believe they can do anything.

People who are experiencing manic episodes often are irritable and easily angered. They may start fights or arguments. They are easily distracted and rarely follow through with their grand plans. They are unable to pay attention to one thing at a time. During a manic episode, they may make foolish decisions and even act recklessly. Wild spending sprees and careless driving are typical behaviors. Their sex drive is unusually high. They may take risks such as having unprotected sex with people they don't know well.

People with serious mania may have hallucinations. They may see, hear, or taste things that aren't really there. People with serious mania also may have delusions, or strange, unreal ideas.

Sometimes people with biploar disorder cannot remember having a manic episode. When they are told about an episode, they may fcel frustrated and confused.

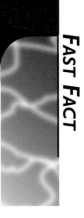

Depression—The Lows

During an episode of depression, people with bipolar disorder may feel sad and empty. Nothing can cheer them up. They may have constant feelings of guilt, worthlessness, and helplessness.

People who are experiencing an episode of depression often feel tired and slowed down. They may lose interest in daily activities and pleasures. They often have difficulty concentrating and making decisions.

Depression can affect a person's physical health. People who are depressed may gain weight or lose weight without trying. They may have aches and pains that are not caused by physical illness or injury. People who are depressed may have difficulty falling asleep or staying asleep.

During an episode of depression, people with bipolar disorder may lose the ability to function in daily life. They may be unable to go to school or to work. They may spend days or weeks in bed. Suicide, or killing themselves, may seem like the only way to escape their emotional pain.

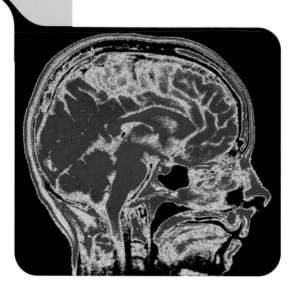

Who Gets Bipolar Disorder?

Bipolar disorder affects up to 3 percent of the population. Almost 3 million people in the United States have this illness. This number does not include teens and children. About 450,000 people in Canada have bipolar disorder.

The illness affects males and females in equal numbers. It can develop at any age. In fact, more and more children are being diagnosed, or identified, with the disease. Usually, however, symptoms, or signs, first appear in the late teens or early twenties. The illness may take several years to develop fully. Often people don't realize they have bipolar disorder because they don't think of the highs as part of the illness. If untreated, bipolar disorder grows worse as the person gets older.

Bipolar disorder tends to run in families. About 80 to 90 percent of people with bipolar disorder have relatives with depression. However, a family history of bipolar disorder does not mean that the illness will develop in every family member. Scientists are working to prove a link between a person's genes, the material that determines characteristics, and bipolar disorder.

Causes of Bipolar Disorder

No one knows the exact cause of bipolar disorder. Brain chemistry, genetics, and environment all seem to have a part.

Two methods have been used to look at the brain of people with bipolar disorder. They are called magnetic resonance imaging (MRI) and positron emission tomography (PET). These methods produce photographic pictures, or scans, of the brain. They show parts of the brain that may not function properly during an episode of mania or depression.

Scientists think that a lack of neurotransmitters may cause the brain malfunction. These chemicals help brain cells communicate with each other. Irregular production of hormones, the chemicals that regulate growth and development, also may play a role. Another possibility is a buildup of calcium in brain cells. This mineral is important in the development and repair of bones and teeth.

An episode of mania or depression may occur for no apparent reason. Other times, something stressful in a person's environment may trigger an episode. It might be a divorce or the death of a loved one. It might be something that seems unimportant, like missing the bus. People with bipolar disorder often are unable to withstand even a small amount of stress. However, bipolar disorder is not a weakness in a person's character. It is a treatable illness.

"My moods are like the pendulum on a grandfather clock. They swing from one extreme to another. Sometimes I feel like I'm going to snap."
—Connor, age 15

Certain medical conditions can bring about manic or depressive episodes. These include a stroke, a brain tumor, or a seizure disorder. A seizure is a sudden, abnormal activity in the brain. Street drugs and prescription medicines also may trigger symptoms of mania and depression.

Effects of Bipolar Disorder

If left untreated, bipolar disorder can destroy a person's life. The extreme mood swings can interfere with the person's ability to go to school or keep a job. People with bipolar disorder may have difficulty keeping friends. They may be viewed as self-centered and untrustworthy. If they behave too wildly, they may get arrested. They may hurt others and themselves.

Bipolar disorder can affect a person's family, too. The person with bipolar disorder may seem to have two personalities. Family members often don't know how the person will act. This can make the family tense and worried. The person with bipolar disorder may argue with family members and be uncooperative. Family members also must cope with the person's serious misbehavior and its consequences.

People with bipolar disorder often don't understand their own behavior. During calm periods, they may feel regret or shame for their actions. They may not know how to get the help they need.

Points to Consider

How might having extreme mood swings create difficulty for a person?

Why would it be helpful to know about family members who have had depression or extreme mood changes?

Do you know anyone who has extreme mood swings? If so, how do you react to this person?

Chapter Overview

The four categories of bipolar disorder are bipolar I, bipolar II, cyclothymia, and bipolar not-otherwise-specified (NOS).

Bipolar I is the most serious form. High and low moods are sharply defined, and mood changes tend to be dramatic.

In bipolar II, episodes of major depression alternate with episodes of hypomania, a milder form of mania.

In cyclothymia, episodes of mild depression alternate with episodes of hypomania.

In all categories of bipolar disorder, episodes of mania and depression vary in pattern, length, and frequency. Cycling refers to the length of time between episodes.

Types of Bipolar Disorder

Bipolar disorder affects the people who have it in different ways. Some have severe symptoms. Others have only mild symptoms. Episodes of depression or mania last a long time in some people, and only a short time in others.

Four Categories of Bipolar Disorder

The American Psychiatric Association divides bipolar disorder into four categories. They are bipolar I, bipolar II, cyclothymia, and bipolar not-otherwise-specified (NOS).

"Sometimes the change from mania to depression hurts. It feels like a knife in my heart. When I'm not manic or depressive, I feel like I'm just waiting for something to happen. Sooner or later something will set off a spark and I'll explode."—Baylor, age 16

Bipolar I

Bipolar I is the most serious form of the illness. A person with bipolar I has manic episodes that are usually followed by periods of major depression. The symptoms last for at least one week. Some people with bipolar I, however, may not have severe depression.

Mixed episodes also may occur with bipolar I. This means that the person has both manic and depressive moods in the same episode. For example, he or she may be restless and energetic while feeling deeply sad.

Severe bipolar I almost always leads to hospitalization. People with bipolar I may become psychotic. This means they lose touch with reality. People with bipolar I also are at high risk for suicide.

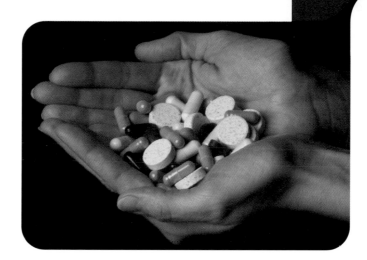

Todd feels happy beyond description. Nothing can stop him. In his mind, he can never fail. He throws himself into his schoolwork. He stays up all night, several nights in a row, writing term papers and working on projects. Ideas and plans fill his head.

When Todd gets like this, he tends to act without thinking. Last week, he charged over $1,000 to his mother's credit card. He didn't think about his not having a job or a way to pay her back.

Four months later, Todd has fallen into a deep, dark hole of sadness. To him, the world seems like a terrible place. Todd's depression started when he got a B on a math test. He expected an A.

Todd has no energy at all. He can hardly pull himself out of bed to go to school. On Friday night, he goes to bed and stays there until Monday morning. He only gets up to go to the bathroom. He cries and wonders why no one understands him. He thinks about swallowing all the pills in the medicine cabinet.

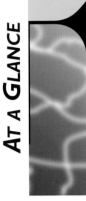
Some experts believe there should be another category of bipolar disorder—bipolar III. This category would include people whose mood changes are caused by drug abuse, medicine, another disease, or a medical treatment.

Todd has bipolar I. His high and low moods are extreme. However, Todd does not have mixed episodes. His moods clearly shift between high and low.

Bipolar II
People with bipolar II have alternating episodes of hypomania and major depression. Hypomania is a milder form of mania in which symptoms last at least four days. Bipolar II also is called hypomania.

People with bipolar II often like the way they feel during episodes of hypomania. They have a high level of energy. Their thinking is clear and sharp. They're able to make decisions easily, and are creative, enthusiastic, and self-confident. They may feel powerful. Other people usually enjoy their company.

Faye has bipolar II. During episodes of hypomania, she is interested in everything. She feels confident and becomes friendly and talkative. During these episodes, Faye takes on more activities than she normally would. She volunteers for everything that comes along and often takes a leadership role.

FAYE, AGE 17

Although episodes of hypomania can seem fairly harmless, people with bipolar II can have extreme behaviors. They may make foolish decisions or act in embarrassing ways. Sooner or later, though, a major depression crushes their good feelings.

People with bipolar II generally do not become psychotic or require hospitalization. If undiagnosed and untreated, however, hypomania can develop into bipolar I.

Cyclothymia

People with cyclothymia have alternating episodes of mild depression and hypomania that last at least two years. To others, these people may seem a little moody or difficult. Often people with cyclothymia will not seek treatment because their mood changes are not extreme. However, about one-third of people with cyclothymia will have bipolar I or bipolar II later in life.

Bipolar Not-Otherwise-Specified (NOS)

Bipolar NOS refers to forms of the illness that do not fit the other three categories. People with bipolar NOS may experience fast changes between manic and depressive episodes. They may have mania or hypomania without depressive episodes. Other disorders such as schizophrenia may co-occur with bipolar NOS. Schizophrenia is a severe mental illness in which the person experiences ongoing hallucinations and delusions. He or she often loses touch with reality.

More About Episodes

The mood changes in bipolar disorder can be rapid and dramatic. Most often they are gradual and not so obvious. Episodes are not always regular or evenly balanced. Some people with bipolar disorder may have several episodes of depression before they have an episode of mania. Others may have only a single episode of mania in their lifetime.

Some people's episodes correspond to the changing seasons. These people may experience depression during the fall and winter months and mania during spring and summer.

Many famous musicians, artists, and writers may have had bipolar disorder. They include author Edgar Allan Poe, artist Vincent Van Gogh, and author Ernest Hemingway. Some think that the energy and drive of the manic phase may have spurred their creative genius.

Cycling

The term *cycling* refers to the length of time between episodes. During the time between highs and lows, the person may feel calm—neither depressed nor manic. However, some people with bipolar disorder may feel mild mania or depression between the highs and lows. Others cycle so fast they never feel calm.

About 20 percent of people with bipolar I and II have rapid cycling. Their high and low moods alternate at least 4 times in 12 months. Rapid cycling often is more difficult to treat.

Some people with bipolar disorder have ultra-rapid cycling. Their mood changes several times within 24 hours. This condition is hard to distinguish from mixed episodes. It also is difficult to treat.

Points to Consider

Why do you think it is helpful to know about different types of bipolar disorder?

Which type of bipolar disorder might be the most difficult to treat? Why?

Why might it be important for someone with bipolar disorder to be hospitalized?

Chapter
Overview

Bipolar disorder can be difficult to diagnose. Psychiatrists and psychologists are the most qualified to diagnose bipolar disorder.

Psychiatrists collect information about a person before making a diagnosis. They request a physical exam and medical history. They conduct psychological tests and interviews with the person and the person's family.

Psychiatrists must rely on their training and experience to make a diagnosis. They also use criteria, or standards, from the American Psychiatric Association to guide their decision.

People with bipolar disorder may go for many years before their illness is correctly diagnosed.

Chapter 3

How Is Bipolar Disorder Diagnosed?

Bipolar disorder can be difficult to diagnose because it is a complex illness that has many forms. Its symptoms resemble those of other illnesses and conditions. To further complicate matters, some illnesses may occur along with bipolar disorder.

"I wasn't diagnosed with bipolar until I turned 15. For years, doctors diagnosed me with illnesses that ranged from blood disease to a brain tumor. Finally I was taken to a psychologist who could look past the physical problems and see what was really wrong."
—Jamal, age 17

Who Can Diagnose Bipolar Disorder?

Psychiatrists and psychologists are the most qualified to diagnose bipolar disorder. These professionals are trained to diagnose and treat mental illnesses. Some specialize in bipolar disorder.

Psychiatrists are medical doctors. They can prescribe medications that can help treat bipolar disorder. Psychologists may work with medical doctors in treating people with bipolar disorder. Clinical social workers and psychiatric nurses also are qualified to help treat the illness.

Symptoms of Bipolar Disorder

When medical professionals diagnose bipolar disorder, they look for certain symptoms. The following are general symptoms of bipolar disorder. They include symptoms of both depression and mania.

Symptoms of Depression

Ongoing sad, worried, or empty mood

Feelings of hopelessness and gloom

Feelings of guilt and worthlessness

Loss of interest or pleasure in ordinary activities

Decreased energy, or a feeling of being tired or slowed down

Difficulty concentrating, remembering, or making decisions

Restlessness or irritability

Sleeping too much or too little

Loss of appetite and weight or increased appetite and weight gain

Ongoing physical pain not caused by an illness or injury

Thoughts of death or suicide, or suicide attempts

Hypergraphia is another symptom of mania. *Hyper* means above and *graphia* means writing. The person becomes fascinated with writing. He or she produces pages and pages of scribblings.

Symptoms of Mania

Increased energy, activity, or restlessness

Excessively elated, or "high," feelings

Extreme irritability

Distracted and confused mood

Racing thoughts and rapid talking

Decreased need for sleep

Unrealistic beliefs in ability and powers

Poor judgment (for example, the person may take on too much work, spend money foolishly, or drive recklessly)

Unusual behavior (for example, the person may start hiding things, neglect personal appearance, or listen to the same piece of music over and over)

Reckless sexual behavior

Quarrelsome, pushy behavior

Hank and Sally Foster don't know what to do. They can no longer deal with their daughter Audra's overpowering moods and strange behavior.

One minute Audra is like a ticking bomb. She blows up at the slightest criticism or misunderstanding. The next minute she is so depressed she can hardly function. She sits in bed, crying for hours. Her parents rejoice when her dark mood lifts. Then Audra's beautiful smile turns to uncontrollable giggles. She talks nonstop and stays up all night writing poetry and dancing.

Audra has had hallucinations. One time she thought she saw angels protecting her. She liked their company, but what came next scared her. She felt worms eating her hands and snakes attacking her feet. She could see dead people with rotting faces and bodies in her room.

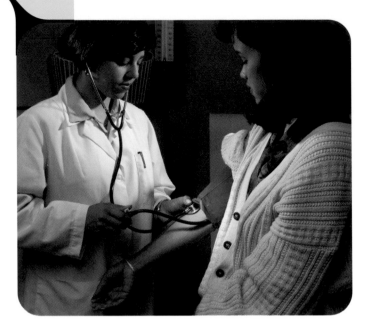

Steps in Diagnosis

There is no simple laboratory test for bipolar disorder. When a person with symptoms of mania and depression seeks help, psychiatrists must use their judgment to diagnose the illness. They first gather information about the person. Then they use the information along with their experience and training to reach a diagnosis.

Psychiatrists go through several steps to gather information. These steps include a physical examination, medical history, interview, and psychological tests.

Physical examination. Psychiatrists request that the person have a physical exam. They need to rule out a physical illness, such as thyroid disease, as the cause of symptoms. The thyroid is a gland that produces hormones that regulate growth. Psychiatrists also try to determine if any medicine the person is taking might be a factor.

Over one-third of people with bipolar disorder say it took 10 years or more to receive a correct diagnosis. People with bipolar disorder generally visit at least three doctors before their illness is diagnosed.

Medical history. The person's medical history provides the psychiatrist with important information. A past illness or injury, especially a head injury, may account for the person's behavior.

The medical history includes information about mental illness in relatives. This is important, because bipolar disorder often has a strong family connection.

AUDRA GETS HELP

Audra's parents were terribly worried. They finally found a psychiatrist they thought could help their daughter. Dr. Rodriguez asked them about other family members who may have had mood disorders.

At first, Mr. and Mrs. Foster couldn't think of anyone. Then Mr. Foster remembered that he had a cousin who had problems with depression. Mrs. Foster mentioned that her sister had a fierce temper and would fly into a rage for no reason. Her grandfather was known for being moody and unpredictable.

Interview. In this step, psychiatrists ask the person about his or her moods and behavior. They may ask about drug abuse and stress in the person's life. They may question the person about relationships. Psychiatrists want to get an idea of the person's baseline personality. This is what the person is like without the symptoms of mania or depression.

FAST FACT

Of the approximately 3 million people in the United States who have bipolar disorder, more than two-thirds are not receiving medical attention. One-fifth of those untreated will kill themselves.

Sometimes the person may be unwilling or unable to provide information. That is why psychiatrists also interview family members. People who are in a manic episode often deny that anything is wrong with them. They may not even remember having manic periods. Family members can describe how the person typically behaves. They also can describe how he or she acts while in a manic or depressed episode. They may be able to recall when symptoms began and how long they lasted.

In the case of children and teens, psychiatrists may interview teachers as well. Play interviews often are done with children. A play interview involves having the child act out experiences or feelings.

Psychological tests. These tests often are used in the diagnosis of bipolar disorder. Psychiatrists require the person to answer multiple-choice questions or explain the meanings of drawings and pictures. Responses to test items may reveal a lot about the person's behavior and moods.

Criteria for Diagnosis

Psychiatrists have an important tool for diagnosing bipolar disorder. They use criteria, or standards, that the American Psychiatric Association (APA) has developed for diagnosing depression and mania. Psychiatrists compare the person's symptoms with the APA's criteria. They compare the number of symptoms, how severe they are, and how long they last. The comparison can show if the person might have a certain type of bipolar disorder. The APA criteria help to make the diagnosis of bipolar disorder the same from doctor to doctor.

Delays in Diagnosis

Many people with bipolar disorder may go years before their illness is correctly diagnosed. One reason is that often the person doesn't report all of the symptoms. This makes it difficult for doctors to identify the illness with certainty. There are other reasons, too.

Many times, family physicians are the first to treat persons with bipolar disorder. They may lack the time or training to diagnose the illness. They may not choose to refer the person to a psychiatrist. Some may try treatment that is ineffective.

Five S's tell why people with mental illness don't seek treatment:

Suffering—they are in too much pain or lack energy

Symptoms—they don't recognize their symptoms or realize they may have an illness

Severity—they don't realize how bad their symptoms are

Support—they lack the means to get help, such as health insurance, or encouragement from family and friends

Stigma—they are ashamed of having a mental illness (this is the biggest S of all)

Sometimes people with bipolar disorder are the greatest obstacle to their treatment. They may not want to see a psychiatrist. Some may lack health care insurance to cover treatment. More likely, however, they fear the stigma, or shame, connected with having a mood disorder. They may believe that having bipolar disorder means they are crazy, weak, or bad. None of this is true. People with bipolar disorder did nothing to cause their illness. Bipolar disorder happens to people, just like cancer or heart disease happens to people.

AUDRA SPEAKS OUT

Audra was diagnosed with bipolar I. Audra and her family are relieved to have a name for her illness. They know that identifying the illness is the first step in treating it.

Audra decided to tell her friends about her bipolar disorder. She told them that it is controllable and nothing to be afraid of. Most of Audra's friends are okay with her illness, although they really don't understand it. They just know that Audra is a kid with some different challenges.

Points to Consider

How can family members and friends help a person with bipolar disorder obtain treatment?

Do you think that some people may have negative views of people with bipolar disorder? If so, what can be done to overcome those views?

Do you think people with bipolar disorder should tell others about their illness? Why or why not?

Chapter Overview

Bipolar disorder can develop in children and young teens.

Symptoms of bipolar disorder in children and young teens may vary from those in adults. Children with bipolar disorder tend to alternate between anger and depression.

Bipolar disorder in children and young teens may resemble attention deficit hyperactivity disorder, conduct disorder, schizophrenia, or drug abuse. It also may be overlooked as normal childhood or teen behavior.

A wrong diagnosis or a delay in diagnosis can have serious consequences for children and teens with bipolar disorder.

Chapter **4**

Bipolar Disorder in Children and Teens

Until recently, doctors rarely diagnosed bipolar disorder in children and young teens. The medical profession believed that the illness mainly affected older teens and adults. This idea is changing. Now doctors realize that problems can begin at an early age. Psychiatrists are looking for ways to improve diagnosis of bipolar disorder in children and teens.

How can you tell normal teen moodiness from a mood disorder? Psychiatrists often begin by asking questions such as the following:

Have you ever gone through a time when you became unusually excited?

Have you ever gone through a time when your mood went up and down quickly?

Have you ever gone through a time when you couldn't sleep at night because you had so much energy?

Vanessa feels as though something has been wrong with her all her life.

VANESSA, AGE 14

As a baby, she cried a lot. Her crying was more like screaming. She hardly slept at all. As a toddler, Vanessa had terrible temper tantrums. She banged her head against the wall and threw things.

Vanessa always seemed to have a dark side. In kindergarten, she drew pictures with black, swirling lines. Her first poem at age 8 was entitled "Why Are You So Sad?" As Vanessa grew older, her angry outbursts continued. By the time she was 12, she felt angry all the time. She flew into a rage for no reason. She broke things. She told her mother that she hated her.

Vanessa feels miserable inside. "Why do I act and feel so awful?" she cries. "Why can't I be like everyone else?"

Symptoms of Bipolar Disorder in Children and Teens

Symptoms of bipolar disorder in children and teens may not be the same as in adults. Instead of feeling excited or happy during a manic episode, children may bounce between anger and depression. Like Vanessa, they may have outbursts of rage. Children with bipolar disorder tend to have physical complaints. They may have frequent headaches and stomachaches.

Children with bipolar disorder may cycle differently from the way adults with the disorder do. Instead of the gradual shifts in mood that adults experience, children's moods may change quickly. Instead of periods of extreme moods, their moods may be continuous.

Diagnosing Bipolar Disorder in Children and Teens

Diagnosing bipolar disorder in children and young teens can be even more difficult than in adults. For one thing, symptoms may be hard to distinguish from normal childhood behavior. Hypomania in children, for example, may seem like childhood enthusiasm. Depression in children may seem like shyness. Mood swings in teens with bipolar disorder may be thought of as typical teen moodiness.

Symptoms of bipolar disorder may resemble symptoms of other illnesses and conditions. For example:

Being easily distracted, impulsive, and overly active are symptoms of attention deficit hyperactivity disorder (ADHD).

Acting violent and aggressive is a symptom of conduct disorder.

Hallucinations and delusions are symptoms of schizophrenia.

Acting high is a symptom of drug abuse.

Doctors may mistake bipolar disorder for one of these other conditions. To make things more confusing, ADHD, conduct disorder, schizophrenia, and drug abuse can exist along with bipolar disorder. Children, teens, and adults all can have these illnesses and conditions.

The Tragedy of Misdiagnosis

Children and young teens who have bipolar disorder may go undiagnosed. They may be misdiagnosed and given a treatment that does not work. The treatment even may make their illness worse.

Misdiagnosis or a delay in diagnosis is unfortunate at any age. It is especially tragic for children and teens. If untreated, children and young teens with bipolar disorder may miss out on important developmental tasks. They may not acquire the social, mental, and emotional skills they will need as adults. Their self-esteem and self-image may be damaged for life.

DID YOU KNOW?

Internationally known author Danielle Steel describes her son's battle with bipolar disorder in *His Bright Light: The Story of Nick Traina.* Nick committed suicide at age 19.

Children and teens with bipolar disorder may endure years of punishment for behavior they cannot control. Classmates may ridicule them. Teens with bipolar disorder may turn to drugs or alcohol to even out their moods. One teen said she started taking drugs to feel normal. She eventually found herself with two problems—drug addiction and bipolar disorder.

Worst of all, children and teens with bipolar disorder may become suicidal. They may see suicide as the only way to end the confusion in their brain. The number of suicide attempts is high among people with bipolar disorder. Depressed teens are especially at risk. They lack experience to cope with the lows of depression. They may act without thinking things through.

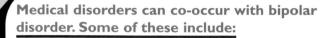

Medical disorders can co-occur with bipolar disorder. Some of these include:

Eating disorders

Severe headaches or migraines

Panic disorder

Muscle and joint pain

Ian, who has bipolar disorder, seemed headed for a life behind bars. Then someone rescued him.

IAN, AGE 15

As a child, Ian was charming and bright. He did well in elementary school, although he seemed hyper at times. If he got an idea in his head, he acted on it immediately. Sometimes he did reckless things, such as walking on the edge of a balcony. His classmates would be horrified and thrilled.

When Ian entered middle school, his illness swung between anger and depression. He misbehaved in class and mouthed off to teachers. He tried not to keep messing up, but he couldn't seem to follow the rules. He was suspended several times for fighting and then finally expelled. The school labeled him a behavior problem.

By the time Ian was 13, he drank alcohol and took drugs. He ran away from home several times and got arrested. The juvenile court judge took a special interest. She ordered psychiatric tests for Ian. Once the court-appointed psychologist diagnosed bipolar disorder, Ian started to get the help he needed.

Getting Help

You may know someone with extreme mood changes or someone who has shown a dramatic change in behavior. That person may have bipolar disorder. You may be worried about your own moodiness. In either case, you must seek help. Talk with a parent, school counselor, family doctor, spiritual leader, or other trusted adult. He or she can help you contact a psychologist, psychiatrist, social worker, or mental health counselor.

If Someone You Know Threatens Suicide

You can help a suicidal person. Take all threats of suicide seriously. Learn the warning signs of suicide. These include the following:

Making threats or comments such as "I'd be better off dead"

Giving away prized possessions

Putting things in order and tying up loose ends

Withdrawing from others

Showing any of the signs of depression, especially feelings of hopelessness and helplessness

Encourage the person to talk about his or her situation and then listen. Sometimes just knowing that someone else cares can prevent a person from committing suicide. Problems also may seem less overwhelming when they are discussed openly.

Ask the person directly if he or she is thinking about suicide. Encourage the person not to be ashamed of suicidal thoughts. Suicidal thinking is a symptom of depression, which is a treatable illness. Say that you will help the person find professional help.

You can find help in several ways. Tell a trusted adult about the situation. The adult can help the person find a mental health professional. You also can call a suicide prevention hot line. One usually is listed on the inside front cover of your local phone book. You also can look under *Suicide Intervention* in the phone book.

If You Feel Suicidal

Don't be afraid to admit that you feel suicidal. Tell your doctor immediately. Also tell family members and close friends so that you have a support system. Inform them about suicide's warning signs.

If you are alone and feel desperate, call 9-1-1. You also might call a suicide prevention hot line. One hot line to call is the Covenant House Nineline (**1-800-999-9999**). The people who answer the phone can provide immediate help to people thinking about suicide.

Points to Consider

What would you do if you tried to get help for bipolar disorder and no one believed you?

Why do you think bipolar disorder can be undiagnosed or misdiagnosed in teens?

What resources are available at your school for students who may have a mental or an emotional illness?

Chapter
Overview

People with bipolar disorder need medication to stabilize their moods. Lithium and divalproex sodium are commonly prescribed medications for bipolar disorder.

Continuing to take medication can be an issue for people with bipolar disorder.

Psychotherapy and support groups can be helpful additions to a treatment program.

People with bipolar disorder who do not improve with medication may have electroshock therapy.

Treatment in a hospital mental health unit may be necessary for some people with bipolar disorder.

How Is Bipolar Disorder Treated?

Bipolar disorder can seriously affect a person's life. However, this does not have to happen. Bipolar disorder is one of the most treatable of all mental illnesses. Proper diagnosis and treatment can help most people with this disease have a better life.

Medications

Medications are the most important part of treatment for bipolar disorder. Medications help to stabilize, or even out, a person's moods. Some people may need many different medications to control their symptoms. Treatment must be tailored to the individual because every person is different.

Lithium and Divalproex Sodium

Lithium and divalproex sodium are mainly effective for controlling mania. They may relieve depression as well. These medications are taken in the form of pills. It may take from four to six weeks for the medications to start working effectively.

People who take lithium or divalproex sodium must have their blood checked regularly. Blood tests show the level of the medication in the bloodstream. Too little lowers the drug's effectiveness. Too much could poison the person. At first, the person's blood is checked one or more times each week. After that it may be checked only monthly. Doctors adjust the dosage according to the results of the blood tests.

Doctors also may adjust the dosage to reduce side effects. Side effects of lithium may include increased thirst and frequent urination, or going to the bathroom. Other side effects are vomiting, or throwing up, and drowsiness. Side effects of divalproex sodium may include some hair loss and nausea, or feeling like throwing up. People on lithium or divalproex sodium may gain weight and feel drowsy. Their hands may tremble. People on divalproex sodium are at a slight risk for liver damage.

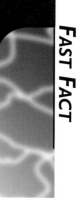
Lithium is effective in 60 to 80 percent of people with bipolar disorder.

Lithium and divalproex sodium are not effective in all cases of bipolar disorder. In these instances, doctors may prescribe other types of drugs. Antipsychotic and antidepressant drugs also are used in the treatment of bipolar disorder. These drugs relieve symptoms of illnesses such as schizophrenia or depression.

The Problem With Compliance

Compliance, or a person's cooperation with the treatment program, is often a problem in bipolar disorder. After being on medication for a while, people with bipolar disorder generally feel much better. They may begin to doubt their need for medication. They may believe they are cured. As a result, they stop taking the drugs. Some people with bipolar disorder quit taking their medication because they dislike the side effects. Others may miss the good feeling of hypomania and believe medication robs them of creativity and energy.

However, most people with bipolar disorder must take medication the rest of their life. Without medication, the person's symptoms soon will return. They may be worse than ever. Episodes of mania and depression may become more dangerous, putting the person's life at risk. If the person decides to go back on medication, the drug may not be as effective.

"My doctor had to get my brain chemistry under control first. Then I was able to concentrate on therapy. My therapist helped me lighten up on myself."
—Brandy, age 16

"My family knew I was in trouble so it was back to the hospital. The doctors there helped me a lot. But it was the other kids who were the greatest comfort. We all understood each other. For the first time, I didn't feel like a freak."—Heather, age 18

WESLEY, AGE 18

Wesley was a freshman in college. He had been on lithium for two years and was feeling normal. He thought he didn't need medication anymore. He believed he was strong enough to do without lithium.

Without telling his doctor, Wesley stopped taking the drug. Things were fine for a while. Then Wesley began to have symptoms of bipolar disorder again. He became wildly manic and then severely depressed.

One night Wesley was alone in his fourth-floor dorm room. He opened the window and crawled out. Wesley hesitated for only a minute before jumping. He died of massive internal injuries.

Psychotherapy

Psychotherapy can be an important supporting treatment for bipolar disorder. However, it cannot take the place of medication. Psychotherapy means talking with a trained therapist. The therapist might be a psychiatrist, psychologist, mental health counselor, or clinical social worker.

A therapist can help a person with bipolar disorder understand the illness and stay with treatment. Bipolar disorder usually causes many problems in a person's life. A therapist can help the person deal with stress, build a positive self-image, and improve personal relationships.

Support Groups

Support groups are another important addition to treatment. These groups are made up of people with similar problems who meet regularly to share experiences. The group members discuss issues related to their illness. They learn and gather strength from each other. Support groups also may include family members and friends of people with bipolar disorder.

Electroshock Therapy

Some people with bipolar disorder do not improve with medication. They may not respond to these drugs. In such situations, doctors may order electroshock therapy, or ECT, which has a high rate of success.

ECT involves passing a small amount of electrical current through the brain. The current moves into the brain through electrodes attached to the person's head. Doctors believe that the electrical current alters the brain's chemistry and relieves depression and mania. Side effects may include headaches, sore muscles, nausea, confusion, and temporary memory loss.

A series of treatments may be needed before symptoms improve. Following electroshock therapy, a person with bipolar disorder usually takes medication to keep the illness under control. The person is hospitalized for several days so doctors can observe the effects of the treatment.

Hospitalization

Sometimes people with bipolar disorder must be admitted to a hospital for treatment. They may be a danger to themselves or others. They also may need to withdraw from alcohol or other drugs. In some cases, they may not be able to care for themselves. After discharge from the hospital, they still will need follow-up treatment.

Mia's doctor started her on medication for bipolar disorder. <u>MIA, AGE 17</u>
The medication didn't help. Mia tried to slit her wrists. It was her fourth suicide attempt in three months. Mia was put in the hospital until the doctor could find the right medication and the right dosage.

Mia felt safe in the hospital. She could let off steam without hurting herself or anyone else. She had time to read and relax and think about her life.

There were other kids in the mental health unit. Mia liked being with others who understood what she was going through. She took part in group talks and some individual therapy. She also did things like arts and crafts. Any other time she might have felt silly making clay figures. At the hospital, she appreciated being able to do something simple.

Points to Consider

Why do you think people with bipolar disorder might resist taking their medication? How might this be dangerous?

As a teen, how would you feel about having to take medication for the rest of your life? What concerns might you have?

How could you help a teen with bipolar disorder stick to his or her treatment plan?

Chapter Overview

Bipolar disorder cannot be cured, but the symptoms can be controlled. People with bipolar disorder can learn to manage their illness.

Taking medication as prescribed is the most important way to control bipolar disorder. Talking with a therapist and attending support group meetings also are important.

People with bipolar disorder can learn to recognize early symptoms. Their medication can be adjusted to prevent mania or depression.

Family members and friends can provide important support to a person with bipolar disorder.

Chapter 6

Staying Healthy

Bipolar disorder is a chronic illness. That means it lasts a long time—usually a lifetime. There is no cure for bipolar disorder. The symptoms, however, can be managed and life can be good. People with this disease can learn what to do to stay healthy.

If You Have Bipolar Disorder

SAMANTHA, AGE 15

Samantha recently began taking lithium for her bipolar disorder. Things aren't perfect, but they're getting better. Samantha doesn't fly into rages anymore. She still gets angry sometimes, but she can talk about her anger now. She occasionally feels sad, but her sadness doesn't overpower her. Samantha can have a calm conversation and be in control of her thoughts. Her mind feels quiet.

Samantha sees a therapist once a week. She is learning to deal with problems in her life and make decisions. She also is learning how to get along better with other people. Samantha can enjoy life again. She laughs and has fun. Best of all, she can sleep at night like other people.

If you are a teen with bipolar disorder, you can do several things to manage your illness. Here are a few suggestions.

Take your medication as prescribed. This is the most important thing you can do. You must take your medicine even when you're feeling well. If you're bothered by side effects, tell your doctor. He or she may be able to adjust your dosage.

Stick with therapy. You don't have to be crazy to go to therapy. Strong, smart people go to therapy to understand themselves better. Therapy can help you understand bipolar disorder and show you new ways to solve your problems.

Pay attention to early symptoms. Learn to recognize when you're becoming depressed or manic. Tell your doctor when you feel an episode coming on or when you don't feel right. Your medication may need adjusting.

Learn everything you can about bipolar disorder. Knowing about your illness will help you manage your symptoms. Read books and watch videos about bipolar disorder. Contact mental health organizations for information. See the Useful Addresses and Internet Sites and the For More Information sections at the back of this book.

Join a support group. The National Depressive and Manic-Depressive Association or the National Foundation for Depressive Illness can give you information about support groups in your area. Their phone numbers are listed in Useful Addresses and Internet Sites at the back of this book.

Involve your family in your treatment program. Having a support system will help you cope with your illness. Ask family members to watch you for symptoms. Ask them to go to support group meetings with you.

Decide who should know about your illness. Your close friends and teachers should be aware of your bipolar disorder. This will help them know how to respond to your mood and behavior changes. Your illness may affect your schoolwork. Tell your teachers if you have difficulty concentrating or working under pressure. They can change assignments to fit your needs.

Stay away from illegal drugs and alcohol. Drugs and alcohol are mood-altering substances. Along with the strong chemicals in your medications, they make a deadly combination.

Stick to a routine. Having regular habits will help keep you on an even course. This includes eating meals at the same time every day and going to bed at the same time every night. Don't take on so many activities that you feel overwhelmed. Pace yourself.

Practice good health habits. If your physical health is good, you are better able to cope with the ups and downs of daily life. Get enough sleep. Loss of sleep can trigger a mood swing. Eat healthy foods. Poor nutrition contributes to depression. Exercise regularly. Vigorous exercise releases natural, feel-good chemicals in your brain.

People with bipolar disorder are not alone. Many people have a chronic illness. They, too, must take medicine to manage their symptoms. For example, people with diabetes must take insulin to control their blood sugar. They will take insulin all their life.

Don't let bipolar disorder take over your life. Develop your talents and interests. Get involved in hobbies, sports, and clubs. Volunteer to help others.

ALEX, AGE 17

Alex is under treatment for bipolar disorder. He's been through a lot. With his commitment to treatment and the support of his friends, he should make it. He's temporarily on a homebound study program. His friends bring his books and assignments to him. They tape-record lectures for him.

Alex isn't allowed to drive right now. His friends sometimes take him to doctors' appointments and to the lab for blood work. They also drive him to support group meetings. Sometimes Alex goes out with his friends. His buddies avoid parties or any place where there might be drugs or alcohol. They don't want to tempt Alex.

Other kids at school remember when Alex was manic. They called him crazy. Alex's friends stick up for him. They tell them that Alex has an illness and that he is getting better.

"One thing you can do is keep a mood journal. I write down every day how I'm feeling. It helps me be aware of my moods. That way I can tell if I'm slipping into depression or mania. I can let my therapist know if I need help."—Lana, age 17

If You Know Someone With Bipolar Disorder

You may have a family member or friend with bipolar disorder. Here are ways you can help.

Become informed about bipolar disorder. Read books written by people who have dealt with the disease. Contact mental health organizations for publications on bipolar disorder. Attend support group meetings for family and friends.

Encourage the person to take medication and stick with therapy. People with bipolar disorder need the love and support of family and friends. Encourage the person to continue with treatment. Remember that medication helps stabilize the person's moods. Therapy teaches ways to behave. Never tease the person about taking medication or embarrass him or her about seeing a therapist.

Watch for symptoms. Be alert for a return of symptoms of mania or depression. Point out the symptoms in a caring way. The person may not be aware of his or her behavior.

Set rules and discuss safeguards for manic periods. Decide things you will do to avoid problems during a manic episode. For example, you might not let the person have credit cards, checkbooks, or car keys. If possible, work out rules and safeguards ahead of time with the person.

Do things with, rather than for, the person. Help the person to build self-esteem and independence. Self-esteem means feeling worthwhile and confident about yourself.

Take care of yourself. You will not be able to help the person if you become stressed out or ill. Take time off from caregiving. Share caregiving responsibilities with others. Find time for relaxation and activities you enjoy.

Points to Consider

Do you know anyone with a chronic illness? What does the person do to keep the illness under control?

What are some of the challenges of having a friend or family member with bipolar disorder?

What can you do to educate yourself and others about this illness?

Glossary

chronic (KRON-ik)—continuing for a long time; a person with a chronic disease or condition may have it throughout life.

cyclothymia (sye-kluh-THY-mee-uh)—a form of bipolar disorder in which mild mania alternates with mild depression

delusion (di-LOO-zhuhn)—a false idea or belief, usually not based in reality

depression (di-PRESH-uhn)—a mood disorder in which a person feels extremely sad, hopeless, and helpless

hallucination (huh-loo-suh-NAY-shuhn)—seeing, hearing, or tasting something that is not really there

hormone (HOR-mohn)—a chemical produced by a gland or tissue; hormones enter the bloodstream and control various body processes.

hypomania (hye-puh-MAY-nee-uh)—a milder form of mania

mania (MAY-nee-uh)—a mood disorder in which the person is extremely excited or irritable

neurotransmitter (nu-roh-TRANS-mi-tuhr)—a chemical produced in the brain that moves messages along nerve cells

psychiatrist (sye-KYE-uh-trist)—a medical doctor who specializes in the diagnosis and treatment of mental illness

psychologist (sye-KOL-uh-jist)—a person who provides testing and counseling to people with mental and emotional problems

psychotherapy (sye-koh-THER-uh-pee)—a type of treatment in which a therapist attempts, through conversation, to help a person

psychotic (sye-KAH-tik)—the state of losing contact with reality

schizophrenia (skit-suh-FREE-nee-uh)—a severe mental disorder in which the person loses touch with reality; a person with schizophrenia has strange thought patterns.

stigma (STIG-ma)—a sense of shame

For More Information

Clayton, Lawrence, and Sharon Carter. *Coping With Depression.* New York: Rosen, 1995.

Cobain, Bev. *When Nothing Matters Anymore: A Survival Guide for Depressed Teens.* Minneapolis: Free Spirit, 1998.

Harmon, Daniel E. *The Tortured Mind: The Many Faces of Manic Depression.* Philadelphia: Chelsea House, 1998.

National Depressive and Manic-Depressive Association. *Living With Manic-Depressive Illness: A Guidebook for Patients, Families, and Friends.* Chicago: National Depressive and Manic-Depressive Association.

Peacock, Judith. *Depression.* Mankato, MN: Capstone Press, 2000.

Wolff, Lisa. *Teen Depression.* San Diego: Lucent Books, 1999.

Useful Addresses and Internet Sites

American Association of Suicidology
4201 Connecticut Avenue Northwest
Suite 408
Washington, DC 20008
www.suicidology.org

American Psychiatric Association
1400 K Street Northwest
Suite 501
Washington, DC 20005
www.psych.org

Canadian Mental Health Association
2160 Yonge Street, 3rd Floor
Toronto, ON M4S 2Z3
CANADA
www.cmha.ca

National Depressive and Manic-Depressive
Association (National DMDA)
730 North Franklin Street
Suite 501
Chicago, IL 60610
1-800-82-NDMDA (1-800-826-3632)
www.ndmda.org

National Mental Health Association
1021 Prince Street
Alexandria, VA 22314-2971
1-800-969-NMHA (1-800-969-6642)
www.nmha.org

Depression.com
www.depression.com
Information on many aspects of depression

Joy Ikelman's Info on Bipolar Disorder
www.frii.com/~parrot/bip.html
Facts about the illness and treatments; includes
information on famous people who have
bipolar disorder.

Suicide Awareness\Voices of Education
(SA\VE)
www.save.org
Information on suicide and links to sites with
further information

Covenant House Nineline
1-800-999-9999

DEPRESSION/Awareness, Recognition, and
Treatment Program
D/ART
1-800-421-4211

National Foundation for Depressive Illness
1-800-248-4344

Index

alcohol, 6, 39, 40, 50, 56
American Psychiatric Association
    (APA), 15, 31
attention deficit hyperactivity disorder
    (ADHD), 37, 38

bipolar disorder
    and the brain, 11
    causes of, 11
    in children and teens, 35–43
    definition of, 5
    diagnosing, 23–33, 35, 37–38
    effects of, 12–13
    in families, 10
    and staying healthy, 53–59
    symptoms of, 10, 36–37, 55
    treating, 45–51
    types of, 6, 15–21
    untreated, 7, 10, 19, 38
    what is it?, 5–13
    who gets it?, 10
bipolar I, 15, 16–18, 32
bipolar II, 15, 18–19
bipolar not-otherwise-specified (NOS),
    15, 20
brain tumors, 12

calcium, 11
compliance, 47
concentration difficulties, 9, 25, 56
conduct disorder, 37, 38
counselors, 41, 48
cycling, 21, 37
cyclothymia, 15, 19

decision-making, 8, 9, 18–19, 25
delusions, 8, 20, 37
depression, 7, 9, 10, 11, 36, 40, 47, 56
    and bipolar I, 16–18
    and bipolar II, 18–19
    and bipolar NOS, 20

    and cyclothymia, 19
    symptoms of, 25, 42
diagnosis, 23–33
    in children and teens, 37–38
    delays in, 31–32, 38
    and misdiagnosis, 38–39
    steps in, 28–30
divalproex sodium, 46–47
driving carelessly, 8, 26
drugs, 6, 12, 18, 29, 37, 38, 39, 40, 50,
    56

eating disorders, 40
electroshock therapy (ECT), 49–50
energy, 6, 8, 17, 18, 26
episodes, 7–9, 11, 12, 20. *See also*
    mood swings
    length of, 7, 15, 20
exercise, 56

family, 10, 12, 29, 30, 56, 58
feeling
    angry, 6, 7, 8, 29, 36, 40, 54
    ashamed, 13, 32, 42
    confident, 18
    confused, 8, 26
    empty, 9, 25
    energetic, 6, 8, 16, 18, 26
    frustrated, 7, 8
    guilty, 9, 25
    happy, 5, 8, 17
    helpless, 9, 41
    hopeless, 5, 25, 41
    irritable, 8, 25, 26
    out of control, 5, 6, 7
    regret, 13
    restless, 8, 16, 25
    sad, 5, 6, 9, 16, 17, 25, 54
    tired, 6, 9, 25, 46
    worthless, 9, 25
friends, 12, 32, 56, 57, 58

Index continued

genes, 10, 11

hallucinations, 8, 20, 27, 37
headache, 36, 40
hormones, 11
hospitalization, 16, 50, 51
hypergraphia, 26
hypomania. *See* bipolar II

interviews, 29–30

lithium, 46–47, 48, 54

magnetic resonance imaging (MRI), 11
mania, 7, 8, 47
    and bipolar I, 16–18
    and bipolar II, 18–19
    and bipolar NOS, 20
    and cyclothymia, 19
    remembering episodes of, 8, 25, 30
    symptoms of, 26, 28
manic depression. *See* bipolar disorder
medical history, 28–29
medications, 24, 28, 45–46, 47, 54, 57, 58
    prescription, 12
mental illness, 29, 32
mood swings, 5, 6, 12, 37. *See also* episodes

National Depressive and Manic-Depressive Association, 55
National Foundation for Depressive Illness, 55
neurotransmitters, 11

panic disorder, 40
physical exams, 28
physical illness, 9, 25, 28, 36
positron emission tomography (PET), 11

psychiatrists, 24, 28–32, 35, 36, 41, 48
psychological tests, 30
psychologists, 24, 41, 48
psychotherapy, 48–49, 51, 55, 58
psychotic, 16

rapid cycling, 21
repeated transcranial magnetic stimulation (rTMS), 50
risk-taking, 8, 17, 26, 40

schizophrenia, 20, 37, 38, 47
seizure disorders, 12
self-esteem, 59
sex drive, 8, 26
sleep problems, 8, 9, 17, 25, 26, 27, 36, 54
social workers, 24, 41, 48
spending sprees, 8, 17, 26
stomachache, 36
stress, 11, 29, 56
strokes, 12
suicide, 9, 16, 17, 25, 30, 39, 41–43, 48, 51
support groups, 49, 51, 55, 56, 57, 58
symptoms, 10, 37, 55, 58
    of depression, 25
    of mania, 26

talking, 41–42
    rapidly, 8, 26, 27
therapists, 48–49, 54
thoughts, 8, 18, 26, 54
treatment, 45–51, 58

ultra-rapid cycling, 21
unipolar disorder, 6

weight loss or gain, 9, 25, 46